CLIFFS NOTES on

$2.95

FITZGERALD'S THE GREAT GATSPY

Cliffs NOTES INC.®

YOUR KEY TO THE CLASSICS

A NOTE TO THE READER

These Notes present a clear discussion of the action and thought of the work under consideration and a concise interpretation of its artistic merits and its significance.

They are intended as a supplementary aid to serious students, freeing them from interminable and distracting note-taking in class. Students may then listen intelligently to what the instructor is saying, and to the class discussion, making selective notes, secure in the knowledge that they have a basic understanding of the work. The Notes are also helpful in preparing for an examination, eliminating the burden of trying to reread the full text under pressure and sorting through class notes to find that which is of central importance.

THESE NOTES ARE NOT A SUBSTITUTE FOR THE TEXT ITSELF OR FOR THE CLASSROOM DISCUSSION OF THE TEXT, AND STUDENTS WHO ATTEMPT TO USE THEM IN THIS WAY ARE DENYING THEMSELVES THE VERY EDUCATION THAT THEY ARE PRESUMABLY GIVING THEIR MOST VITAL YEARS TO ACHIEVE.

These critical evaluations have been prepared by experts who have had many years of experience in teaching the works or who have special knowledge of the texts. They are not, however, incontrovertible. No literary judgments are. There are many interpretations of any great work of literature, and even conflicting views have value for students and teachers, since the aim is not for students to accept unquestionably any one interpretation, but to make their own. The goal of education is not the unquestioning acceptance of any single interpretation, but the development of an individual's critical abilities.

The experience of millions of students over many years has shown that Notes such as these are a valuable educational tool and, properly used, can contribute materially to the great end of literature (to which, by the way, the teaching of literature is itself only a subsidiary)—that is, to the heightening of perception and awareness, the extending of sympathy, and the attainment of maturity by living, in Socrates' famous phrase, "the examined life."

THE GREAT GATSBY

NOTES

including
- *Introduction*
- *Life of Fitzgerald*
- *Brief Synopsis*
- *List of Characters*
- *Chapter Commentaries*
- *Notes on Characters*
- *Critical Review*
- *Review Questions*
- *Selected Bibliography*

by
Phillip Northman, M.A.
Department of English
Memphis State University

NEW EDITION

INCORPORATED
LINCOLN, NEBRASKA   68501

Editor

Gary Carey, M.A.
University of Colorado

Consulting Editor

James L. Roberts, Ph.D.
Department of English
University of Nebraska

NEW EDITION
ISBN 0-8220-0560-3
© Copyright 1966
by
C. K. Hillegass

Cliffs Notes, Inc.   Lincoln, Nebraska

CONTENTS

INTRODUCTION 5

THE LIFE OF F. SCOTT FITZGERALD 7

BACKGROUND OF THE 1920's 12

LIST OF CHARACTERS 15

CHAPTER COMMENTARIES

Chapter I 16
Chapter II 20
Chapter III 22
Chapter IV 25
Chapter V 28
Chapter VI 30
Chapter VII 34
Chapter VIII 37
Chapter IX 39

NOTES ON MAIN CHARACTERS

Nick Carraway 42
Jay Gatsby 43
Daisy Buchanan 44
Tom Buchanan 45
Jordan Baker 45

CRITICAL REVIEW

Ideas 46
Settings 46
Technique and Structure 47
Style 49
Symbolism 50

REVIEW QUESTIONS 51

SELECTED BIBLIOGRAPHY 53

INTRODUCTION

These Notes are in no way intended to serve as a substitute for the actual reading of *The Great Gatsby*. Though they will be useful as a review, they are designed mainly to give the reader an increased understanding and enjoyment of the novel. The intelligent use of the Notes, combined with a careful study of the text itself, should provide a richer comprehension of the elements that have made *The Great Gatsby* a finished work of art.

One feature that distinguishes the classics of our literature is the conscious artistry that fuses a work into a unified whole; every detail contributes to the unity of the final product, and nothing superfluous is permitted to remain. *The Great Gatsby* possesses this unity to a high degree, and this is a major reason for its survival as an important American novel rather than as a mere historical document depicting life in the twenties.

Because of the importance of careful construction in attaining artistic unity, one of the main objectives of the critical commentary is to point out the significance of seemingly unimportant details. The colors of things, the location of the action, and even the weather are important in a way that they are not in reality, since they all contribute on more than one level to the unity of the novel. However, no amount of explication can exhaust all the significance of every detail, and ultimately it will be the reader's task to piece together the many aspects of the novel and actively recreate in his mind a final version of his own. In a very real sense this is a creative act, and as such it is extremely rewarding. The Notes are designed to help stimulate the reader's mind toward developing this capacity, by discussing some of the aspects and significances of a limited number of the novel's details.

Important as content is, however, it is *form* that shapes the novel's unity, until ultimately the form and the content become inseparably united in an artistic whole. Of all Fitzgerald's novels, *The Great Gatsby* shows the greatest consciousness of form in its construction, and this is the main reason it is considered the best of his works today. Here again, the Notes will help the reader come to his own understanding of the novel's art, by pointing out some of the intricacies of the narrative structure such as chronology, juxtaposition, and point of view.

Fitzgerald's method of narration illustrates the importance of form. One of the numerous consequences of using Nick Carraway as a first-person narrator is that the immediacy of the presentation is increased, making the whole novel more dramatic. Fitzgerald himself once said of *The Great Gatsby* that everything must contribute to the dramatic movement, and the device of a first-person narrative is one of the ways in which this objective is attained. However, as a main character taking part in the novel's action, Nick becomes far more than just a narrative device. On one level, the action of *The Great Gatsby* is the story of what happens to Nick, and the conclusions he draws from his experiences make up a large part of the book's thematic material. Thus the role of the narrator is very important both in terms of formal structure and thematic content.

Despite its brilliant description of Jazz Age America and its equally skillful characterization, *The Great Gatsby* is primarily a novel of ideas. There is a heavy reliance on symbolism throughout the book, since by its very nature a symbol functions on several levels at once, fitting into the action at the same time as it represents an idea. There is an abundance not only of such physical symbols as the green light on Daisy's dock or the eyes of Dr. T. J. Eckleburg, but symbolic action as well. Moving from west to east, for example is always symbolic of the moral situation of the characters, and the peculiar way Gatsby smiles or Tom Buchanan moves illustrates important aspects of their personalities. In fact, Gatsby's whole career is finally made into a metaphor for the entire American experience. In considering the novel's symbolism the reader may find the Notes especially useful; with some of the symbols identified as he progresses through the book, his comprehension of the controlling ideas should be accelerated.

As a work of art *The Great Gatsby* is able to stand on its own merits, independent of the need for explanation in terms of the author's life or the cultural milieu in which it was created. However,

Fitzgerald's own life has more direct pertinence to his work than the lives of most writers, and for this reason a brief biography is included in the prefatory material to the Notes.

In *The Great Gatsby* as well as in virtually all of Fitzgerald's writing, the subject of wealth occupies a central position, as it did in the author's own life. Much of his energy was dedicated to achieving material success, a fact which made him rather suspect among academicians and which led him to consider himself a kind of failure when he was no longer making much money. Partly because of his personal compulsion to make more and more money, Fitzgerald was always preoccupied with the life of the wealthy. Despite his clear realization of their moral corruption, he also had a naive fascination with, and even admiration for, the rich. This comes out in *The Great Gatsby* in such passages as the rather nostalgic description of Daisy's "white girlhood" in Chapter VIII. In a limited way, Daisy is like Zelda Fitzgerald in that she must be won with evidence of material success, and Fitzgerald is like Gatsby, the "poor" boy who must somehow make enough money to win the "golden girl" of his dreams.

Yet at the same time that Fitzgerald envied the life of the privileged classes he also had the ability to see its emptiness, and these two aspects of his personality are reflected in the central characters of *The Great Gatsby*. While Gatsby is possessed by the magical fascination of wealth, Nick is able to see clearly into the self-destructive nature of that fascination. This splitting-off of Fitzgerald's own ambivalent attitude accounts for much of the novel's success, since it enables the author to set up two opposing sets of values without excessive confusion or ambiguity. That Fitzgerald is able to perceive and objectify the values which he adopted at least partially in his own life is evidence of his insight and artistic integrity.

THE LIFE OF F. SCOTT FITZGERALD

Francis Scott Key Fitzgerald was born on September 24, 1896, in St. Paul, Minnesota, the only son of an upper-middle class

Catholic family. Like Nick Carraway, he had family roots that went deep into "respectable" middle western traditions, at least on the side of his mother, who had inherited a substantial amount of money from a grandfather who had become successful in the wholesale grocery business in St. Paul. His father was a kindly southerner of vaguely aristocratic lineage who never quite managed to succeed in business, moving his family first to Buffalo, New York, then to Syracuse and back again to Buffalo, returning finally in 1908 to St. Paul without having made much money.

Thus the young Scott grew up in the kind of environment that has been characterized as "shabby genteel." His family had the traditions of the upper classes but not the financial security to support those traditions, and while he associated with the children of the rich, he was aware that he was never wholly a part of their society. Perhaps this is the basis of his lifelong devotion to both material and social success; even as a boy he was driven more than most children to try to establish himself by athletics, personal popularity, and ultimately, literary expression. By 1910, in his second year at the St. Paul Academy, he was publishing fiction in the school magazine, an activity he was to continue at prep school and Princeton.

In 1911 he returned to the east to prep at the Newman Academy, a Catholic school in New Jersey. Here Fitzgerald tried desperately hard to distinguish himself at athletics but found he was better suited to achieving success in literary endeavors, publishing three stories in the *Newman News*. He also went on excursions to New York City to see musical comedies and developed an interest in drama that soon led to writing plays of his own. His dramatic efforts were rewarded during the two summers before he went to Princeton, when he saw his plays successfully produced by a local drama club.

Entering Princeton in 1913, Fitzgerald's acute powers of observation began to store up details of the atmosphere he was to recreate in his first novel, *This Side of Paradise*. He immediately began to write for the campus humor magazine, the *Tiger*, and composed lyrics for musical comedies produced by the Triangle. He also published material in the *Nassau Lit.*, a serious literary magazine edited by Edmund Wilson, who was later to become one of America's most distinguished men of letters and a formidable literary critic. Throughout his career Fitzgerald had great respect for the opinions of Wilson, and when he died, Wilson edited his unfinished novel, *The Last Tycoon*, as well as the collection of essays and personal material published as *The Crack-Up* (1945).

While Fitzgerald's literary efforts brought him the recognition he so much desired, his extracurricular activities ruined his grades, and in the winter of 1915 he withdrew temporarily from Princeton on the partial pretext of ill health. At this time his romance with a flighty society girl named Ginerva King had begun to disintegrate, and he entered a difficult period of his life. Like Daisy Fay, Ginerva belonged to the established rich class of Chicago, and as such she was unattainable for Fitzgerald. He returned to Princeton in 1916, and his junior year was marked by the termination of the romance and a shift in his literary interests toward more serious writing, particularly poetry.

By the time of his senior year the war had captured his imagination, and so he left Princeton for an army commission as a second lieutenant in November, 1917. His romantic desire to experience combat is reflected in Nick's remarks about the war in the opening of *The Great Gatsby* as well as in the details of Gatsby's own army career, but Fitzgerald was sent to Alabama instead of Europe. There he began his first novel, originally titled *The Romantic Egoist,* and met Zelda Sayre. She was lovely, daring, and completely undisciplined, the darling of a wealthy Alabama family. Fitzgerald wanted to marry her immediately, but though she loved him she was unwilling to marry anyone who couldn't support her. Therefore, after his discharge in February of 1919 Fitzgerald set out to earn his bride as a writer in New York City.

For eight months he was bitterly disappointed. Forced to work for ninety dollars a month as a writer of advertising copy, he was soon decorating his one-room apartment with rejection slips for the diverse materials he wrote in his off hours, and Zelda remained adamant in her refusal to marry him until he could demonstrate his success. Finally he decided to return to St. Paul, immuring himself in his room to rework the novel he had written in his army days.

When Scribner's accepted the novel for publication in September of 1919, Fitzgerald's success was immediate and spectacular. Magazines began buying his short stories as fast as he could produce them, and in November Zelda consented to be his wife. They were married in April of 1921, and by then *This Side of Paradise* was already in its second printing. It was all a fairy tale come true; he had achieved almost instant financial success and won the girl of his dreams. He became the "golden boy" of American letters, the gifted young genius whose writings typified the new era in American history known as the "Roaring Twenties."

Soon after, Scribner's published a collection of his short stories titled *Flappers and Philosophers,* and the Fitzgeralds moved into a luxury apartment in New York City. There they were the center of a wild, carefree society in which gin flowed like water and money flowed like gin. Fitzgerald paid the bills by writing short stories and somehow found the time to complete his second novel, *The Beautiful and Damned,* which was first serialized and then published in book form in April, 1922. Meanwhile he and Zelda had taken a brief trip to Europe, and Zelda had given birth to their daughter "Scottie" shortly after they returned.

The sales of the second novel were substantial but still disappointing to Fitzgerald. He needed money to maintain their lavish standard of living, and despite a second collection of short stories titled *Tales of the Jazz Age,* he was having trouble meeting expenses. In October of 1922 he and Zelda moved to Great Neck, Long Island, a community that was alive with riotous parties. Here Fitzgerald began his third and finest novel, and it is the atmosphere of Great Neck that one finds in *The Great Gatsby.* For financial support he was depending on the success of his play *The Vegetable, or From President to Postman,* a farce which flopped in Atlantic City in November of 1923. To work himself back into solvency he forced himself to write short stories at a tremendous pace, and his facility soon brought him out of the red, at least for a while.

The following spring the Fitzgeralds moved to Europe, where he continued working on his new novel, and she had an affair with a French naval aviator; both drank more heavily than ever. With a greater sense of conscious artistry than ever before, Fitzgerald strove to make *The Great Gatsby* everything he wished it to be, and when the novel was ready for publication in April of 1925 he predicted it would be a huge popular success. It finally appeared to the most impressive critical appraisals he had ever received, including a letter from T. S. Eliot calling it "the first step American fiction has taken since Henry James" (reprinted in *The Crack-Up*). Edith Wharton, Gertrude Stein, and a host of the foremost writers of the generation lauded the new novel but people failed to buy it, and to Fitzgerald's great disappointment it sold only half as many copies as *The Beautiful and Damned*. After *The Great Gatsby*, he was not to publish another novel until 1934, when Scribner's brought out *Tender Is the Night*.

In the intervening nine years Fitzgerald went into a state of literary eclipse, writing short stories and Hollywood scenarios, and witnessing the skyrocketing career of his friend Ernest Hemingway. He lived sometimes in Europe and other times in America, and his already chronic dependence on alcohol increased. Zelda, who had never been very stable to begin with, became obsessed with a desire to become a professional ballerina; by 1931 her instability progressed into schizophrenia, and she had to be permanently institutionalized. Fitzgerald himself came to be popularly regarded as a literary has-been whose career had ended with the twenties.

Since about 1925 he had been working intermittently on *Tender Is the Night*, which became a mild best-seller for a few weeks after its publication in 1934. Altogether, though, the novel sold even fewer copies than *The Great Gatsby*, despite some very favorable reviews. Under financial pressure, Fitzgerald returned to Hollywood in 1937 for his third try at writing movie scripts. His salary there enabled him to keep Zelda in good psychiatric clinics and helped him pay some of the large personal debt he had accumulated. While in Hollywood he met a twenty-eight-year-old British girl named Sheila Graham, who had risen from the London slums to become a Hollywood newspaper correspondent. She helped him fight his alcoholism and seems to have given him a good deal of support in his last years.

The Last Tycoon, begun in 1939, is a novel based on Fitzgerald's experiences in Hollywood, but no more than a third of it was completed when he suffered his first heart attack in November of 1940. In December a second attack suddenly ended his life. Zelda lived on as an invalid and was burned to death in a sanitarium fire in 1947.

At the time of Fitzgerald's death he was an almost forgotten figure. When the Modern Library dropped *The Great Gatsby* from its lists in 1939, not one of his books remained in print. Then a few critical and appreciative essays began to appear, and in 1945 Edmund Wilson edited *The Crack-Up,* a collection of autobiographical essays, excerpts from Fitzgerald's notebooks, letters, and critical commentary by other writers. In more recent years his reputation has been growing steadily, especially in the last decade. Earlier there had been a tendency to identify his works with the period they characterized, whereas today, with the advantage of a more distant perspective, critics have come to recognize that Fitzgerald merely used the materials of his environment to create literary works which have earned a permanent place in American literature.

BACKGROUND OF THE 1920's

Division of the past into convenient "periods" reflects more expediency than reality. Although pivotal events may be chosen to demarcate phases of historical or literary activity, the divisions tend to obscure the actual gradations and overlapping that occur. The decade of the 1920's—particularly in the United States—came closer to having a sharply defined uniqueness than most recognized periods. World War I inflicted a mortal blow upon the comfortable old world of European culture. The stock market crash in October, 1929, extinguished forever the bright lights and levity of the twenties. In the grim darkness of the Great Depression that followed, nothing survived of the madcap period except memories that took on an almost legendary aura.

Hostilities had been raging for almost three years when the United States actively entered World War I. America had been involved in the conflict little more than a year and a half when it came to an end. The slaughter, horrors, and privations had left all European belligerents weary and spiritually numbed. For America, on the other hand, peace came just as the powerful nation was undergoing a tremendous upsurge in strength and martial fervor.

The entire economy had been regulated to support the huge forces under arms, and the population had been regimented to serve that end. Immoderate measures had been invoked that aroused the people to patriotic excesses. Consequently, the Armistice found the nation possessed of might and suppressed energy, and in the mood for hysteria. Repression and reaction had been the order of the times, and protest and violence followed naturally. National Prohibition and the "witch hunts" that labeled all dissidents as "Reds" provided fuel to keep the caldron boiling.

Never was a time more ripe for literature to defy the canons of the past and boldly and confidently to express the temper of an age. The period before the war had been regarded as dull by restive spirits. Popular writers such as Henry James and Edith Wharton were admired as exemplary champions of the "Genteel Tradition." William Dean Howells was a respected patriarch of American letters. While he earnestly preached realism, Howells doggedly practiced an evasive prudery in his work. The nineteenth-century legacy of "elegance" and "refinement" continued its stifling influence during the pre-war years. But in the tempestuous aftermath of the holocaust, many cherished standards and taboos were swept away, and writers acted precipitously to unfetter literature during the general upheaval. The watchword of the twenties became "civilized," which was supposed to denote an emancipated stance that rose above the handicaps of all previous generations.

However, although literature appeared to burst from its bonds with alarming audacity immediately after World War I, a mood of rebellion had been seething for release during the first two decades of the century. When H. L. Mencken and George Jean Nathan took over the *Smart Set* in 1914, that magazine began its relentless attacks upon the citadels of respectability and enchanted the young with its strident iconoclasm. Mencken's *The American Language*, which appeared in 1919, encouraged writers to cast off the shackles that had restrained the freedom of language. That new attitudes toward the representation of sex were emerging could be seen as early as Stephen Crane's *Maggie: A Girl of the Streets* (1893) and Dreiser's *Sister Carrie* (1900). By 1920, the influence of Freudian psychology lent strong support to this trend.

An element in the transition of American literature had been a metamorphosis in the concept of the nation's past. It had once been taken on trust that life in small towns and rural areas was invariably conducive to human dignity and elevation of the spirit. But later the conviction developed that this kind of salubrious moral climate was only to be found during the early pioneering periods, a phase celebrated in such works as Willa Cather's *O Pioneers!* (1913) and *My Antonia* (1918).

Gradually the grimier side of small-town and rural America became conspicuous. Writers not taken in by the established myth became convinced that the sturdy and upright qualities attributed to pioneer society might utterly perish during the subsequent stage of stable, humdrum life. So the virtues inculcated by a harsh and challenging existence would be displaced by a myriad of their opposites: pettiness, intolerance, greed, hypocrisy—all thriving in an atmosphere of the most abject dullness. Edgar Lee Masters' *Spoon River Anthology* (1915) and Sherwood Anderson's *Winesburg, Ohio* (1919) are testimonials to this rejection of self-deception.

This deflation of the rural-America illusion constituted a distinct movement sometimes referred to as the "Revolt from the Village." A corollary of the movement was an urge on the part of writers for "departure," both as a theme in their works and as a fact in their lives—first, from the confines of the small community and, later, away from American shores. So many writers departed for Europe after the war that they formed a class known as the "expatriates." During the exodus, residence abroad came to be looked upon as almost a requisite for artistic and individual development.

LIST OF CHARACTERS

(In Order of Appearance)

Nick Carraway
    The narrator and moral arbiter of *The Great Gatsby*.

Tom Buchanan
    Who represents the brutality and moral carelessness of the established rich.

Daisy Fay Buchanan
    Nick's distant cousin and Tom's wife. She is the "Golden Girl" who has become the incarnation of Gatsby's dream.

Jordan Baker
    An attractive young woman golfer who becomes involved with the narrator and who is given to compulsive lying.

Jay Gatsby
    Both a racketeer and a romantic idealist, he devotes his life to amassing the wealth he thinks will win Daisy and thereby make his dream come true.

George Wilson
    The proprietor of a shabby garage in the "valley of ashes." His wife is Tom's mistress and he is the deluded killer of both Gatsby and himself.

Myrtle Wilson
    A woman of ludicrous ostentation, whose animal "vitality" attracts Tom and eventually leads to her death.

Catherine
    Myrtle's heavily made-up sister, "a slender, worldly girl of about thirty."

Mr. and Mrs. McKee
    A photographer and his wife, who live in an apartment below the one Tom keeps for Myrtle.

"Owl-Eyes"

A stout, middle-aged man who attends Gatsby's parties and turns up at his funeral.

Meyer Wolfsheim

The Jewish gambler and racketeer who is Gatsby's business associate.

Ewing Klipspringer

The piano-playing "boarder" at Gatsby's house. He is more interested in recovering his gym shoes than in attending Gatsby's funeral.

Dan Cody

A "pioneer debauchee" who employed the youthful Gatsby and gave him his "singularly appropriate education."

Mr. Sloane

He and his lady friend snub Gatsby one afternoon when they stop at his house with Tom.

Michaelis

A young Greek who operates a coffee shop next door to Wilson's garage.

Pammy Buchanan

Tom and Daisy's daughter. She appears momentarily as a possession to be displayed.

Henry C. Gatz

Jay Gatsby's father. A solemn, helpless old man who takes pride in his son's prosperity.

CHAPTER COMMENTARIES

CHAPTER I

The appearance of Nick Carraway as the first-person narrator of *The Great Gatsby* represents a new step in Fitzgerald's fictional technique. Nick helps to give the book a high degree of economy and dramatic intensity by having all the action filtered through his own consciousness and presented in retrospect through his memory. Yet he is much more than a narrative device, since the author is careful to involve him in the plot to the point where he becomes second only to Gatsby in importance, emerging as the only character who had undergone any significant personality development. Nick's limited involvement puts him in a position to report events fully and directly, while remaining enough outside the main action to evaluate these events. As he says of himself later in Chapter II, he is "both within and without," and his dual status as both narrator and a functioning character accounts for a large part of the success with which Gatsby's story is told.

The opening paragraphs reveal Nick's basic qualities as a moralist and a human being. Though he is sensitive to the "fundamental decencies" and interested in keeping the world at a "uniform... moral attention," he is also endowed with a tendency to reserve judgments. This latter quality allows him to become involved with such people as Gatsby, the Buchanans, and Jordan Baker, while the former qualities compel him to come to an ultimate personal judgment of the other characters. His evolution from a position of moral non-involvement to that of definitely judging those about him constitutes Nick's development, which is thus a process of maturing and assuming personal, moral responsibility.

Nick's Scotch ancestry and long-established roots in the middle west are the historical basis of his moral capacity. Tom, Daisy, Jordan, and especially Gatsby all lack such established traditions or have broken with them by permanently moving east, and their consequent lack of a firm moral basis is symbolized by the way they drift aimlessly from place to place or party to party. When Nick moves east, attracted by the false values of wealth and sophistication, his own moral sense is held in abeyance, and when his responsibility finally asserts itself he goes back to the middle west, symbolically returning to a world of moral order based on personal tradition.

His move to West Egg and the subsequent comparison of this location with fashionable East Egg bring up the favorite Fitzgerald theme of the effects of wealth. West Egg is the home of the *nouveaux riches,* of Gatsby and those like him who have made huge fortunes but who lack the traditions associated with inherited wealth and are therefore vulgar. The East Eggers, represented by the Buchanans, have the inherited traditions and lack the vulgarity, but they have been corrupted by the purposelessness and ease their money has provided. Thus both kinds of wealth result in similar human deficiencies, though manifested differently. This is why East Egg and West Egg, superficially so dissimilar, are physically identical when seen from a proper perspective; literally, they are alike as eggs.

The homes of the central characters are indicative of the distinctions of wealth. The Buchanans live in a Georgian Colonial mansion which represents established affluence, while Gatsby owns a pretentious imitation of a European structure, complete with brand-new ivy. Lacking any tradition of his own, Gatsby copies those of others, in the same manner as an American university that erects a library modeled after a medieval Gothic chapel. Nick, the only middle-class character in the book, rents a modest middle-class bungalow flanked by the palaces of the rich, a situation symbolic of his own status in the east.

The events at the dinner party begin to establish the personalities of Tom and Daisy, and Jordan is introduced. Like all the characters besides Nick, the Buchanans never change or develop, though their early outlines are filled in as more information about them is presented. Their lack of development is possibly the reason so much physical detail about them is presented, whereas Nick tells relatively little about his own appearance. Tom and Daisy are static representations, and every physical detail contributes to the construction of their personalities. The arrogant, forceful postures of Tom's "cruel body," his glistening boots, and his manner of shoving other people around all add to the portrait of his self-engrossed brutality, as does his first recorded statement, "I've got a nice place here." Daisy's airy quality as she "floats" on the couch is a clue to her basic insubstantiality, the inner emptiness that is behind all her charming, meaningless gestures.

The dinner party itself is an example of Fitzgerald's dramatic technique, as are the more elaborate parties of the subsequent chapters. Though much of the action is of necessity narrated by Nick, the author gives vividness and immediacy to the high points of the action by presenting them as they happen, rather than merely telling about them through Nick. After a certain amount of conversation that is revealing in its inanity, Tom is called to the telephone (a standard dramatic device), and Nick learns the first significant fact about the Buchanans: Tom has a mistress. This information belies the grace and sophistication of the scene and introduces the theme of adultery which motivates the plot.

The seemingly inconsequential conversation is also illustrative of the Buchanans' way of life. Daisy wants to plan something but doesn't know how to go about it; she needs to have someone decide for her. As Nick remarks earlier, she and those like her are on a "permanent move," drifting aimlessly among the rich with no apparent purpose. With unlimited wealth and without inner resources, her life is as purposeless as the candles that burn on her dinner table in the middle of June. There are "gay, exciting things" in her past and future, but she has no capacity for living in the present.

Tom's secondhand "scientific stuff" indicates his understandable concern for preserving the social status quo. He fears that the lower orders will arise and usurp his women, which foreshadows the fact that Gatsby, a creature of those orders, will soon threaten Tom's domestic status quo by trying to relieve him of his wife.

Jordan is set aside for later development. It is only established that she is very much a part of Tom and Daisy's world, since she is like Tom in that she is an amateur athlete and like Daisy in her place of origin and her first appearance on the couch, though she is actually quite different in physical detail. Throughout the novel Jordan seems to have no fixed abode, constantly drifting like the others.

Returning home, Nick catches his first glimpse of the mysterious Gatsby, who is described in a passage as important as it is brief. At the opening of the chapter Nick has revealed that Gatsby is the one person exempt from his unfavorable judgment. Distinguished by his extraordinary, romantic capacity for hope and wonder, Gatsby has a basic spirituality that enables him to construct and preserve a vision, and he "turns out all right" despite the "foul dust" that preys on his dreams. A basic concern of the novel is in revealing the substance behind these generalities, exposing what the dream is and what has destroyed it.

Here Gatsby appears in the attitude of a worshiper, alone and stretching his arms toward the single, faraway green light that is the visible symbol of his vision. Green is the color of promise, of hope and renewal, and ultimately the green light at the end of the first chapter is made parallel to the "green breast of the new world" at the end of the last, fusing Gatsby's vision with that of the explorers who discovered the promise of a new continent. What ultimately "preys on" the vision, the end or goal, is that in America and by Gatsby it can only be attained by the acquisition of material possessions, and so the means corrupt the end and the sacred green light becomes nothing more than a bulb burning at the end of Daisy Buchanan's dock.

CHAPTER II

The first chapter closes with the symbol of Gatsby's dream, and the second opens with the symbol for the "foul dust" that destroys it. The valley of ashes represents the modern world, which, like Eliot's is a "waste land," a grotesque hell created by modern industry, which sends the railroad cars full of ashes, poisoning the American landscape with waste produced in the manufacture of wealth. It is a physical desert that represents the spiritual desolation of modern society.

Overlooking the scene are the gigantic, sightless eyes of Dr. T. J. Eckleburg, which George Wilson later identifies with God. But if these are the eyes of God, it is a God who is no longer present and who was created by the desire of an ambitious oculist to make money. Dim and shabby, the eyes brood over a world that has become a dumping ground. A few paragraphs later they have their human counterpart in the light blue eyes of George Wilson, a shabby, spiritless denizen of the waste land.

In one form or another the ashes pervade the chapter, recurring as the dust on Wilson's wrecked Ford, the ashen veil on his hair and clothing, and the heavy white powder on Catherine's face. The symbolic ashes of spiritual desolation create the "smoky air" at the party in the New York apartment.

The entire second chapter has almost nothing to do with Gatsby directly, containing only a few lines of wild speculation about his past that serve to heighten the mystery that surrounds him. Instead, Fitzgerald provides a full-scale exposition of Tom Buchanan's hypocrisy, selfishness, and brutality. Here again the method is primarily dramatic; Tom, Nick, and the supernumeraries are assembled at a chaotic debauch and allowed to reveal themselves directly to the reader.

Nick is surprised that Tom keeps his mistress quite openly and that all his acquaintances acknowledge the relationship. This, coupled with Tom's insistence that the hesitant Nick must meet the woman, shows the man's attitude toward Myrtle; she is like his horses, another possession to be displayed for the gratification of his own ego. When Tom breaks her nose for chanting Daisy's name, it is not a defense of his wife's honor, but simply a sign of brutality and hypocrisy. If he actually cared about Daisy's honor he wouldn't be openly involved with a mistress in the first place.

Tom's attitude toward Myrtle's husband is similar to the way he later feels about Gatsby. Both men are so far beneath him that he feels free to treat them with open contempt, and his brutality is especially evident in the way he baits the impoverished Wilson in regard to a car he has no real intention of selling. Yet in the end both Gatsby and George Wilson are men of larger spirit than Tom, for Gatsby is selfless in his attitude toward Daisy, and Wilson reacts to the loss of his wife with a show of grief that reveals a love beyond Tom's capacity.

Except for a brief entrance when she is killed, Myrtle's appearance is confined to this chapter, yet she emerges as the best drawn of the minor characters. Her one thought is to escape her class, a desire that results in ludicrous affectation as well as moral confusion. She is obsessed by appearances and unaware of realities, as is shown by her excessive concern for clothing. Marrying her husband on the assumption that he was a gentleman, she found out this wasn't true because he was married in a borrowed suit. Conversely, she was immediately taken by Tom's appearance and first went off with him primarily because of his dress suit and patent leather shoes.

The vulgarity of Myrtle's affectations and the extent of her moral confusion are both funny and pathetic. About to buy a puppy, she hesitates to use the word "bitch" in front of the man who is keeping her, and later she complains about "the shiftlessness of the lower orders" from which she obviously comes. The list of all the things she wants to get illustrates her distorted sense of values: a dog collar, a trick ashtray, and a wreath for her mother's grave all have equal value in her mind. She is a perfect match for Tom in her single-minded, selfish desires.

That Nick allows himself to become involved with these people, despite his objections and his desire to leave, shows that he is indeed reserving his judgment and has yet to arrive at a full moral responsibility. Yet even here he demonstrates his desire to bring order to the moral chaos of the party by one small gesture — when he troubles to wipe a spot of lather from the cheek of the drunken photographer, McKee.

Artistically, the action of the party is a careful study in increasingly drunken perception. Things begin to seem a bit out of focus, like the photograph that seems at first to feature a hen sitting on a rock, and Catherine's homemade eyebrows give a "blurred" effect to her face. Soon time begins to pass in jumps, people disappear and reappear in a drunken haze, and toward the end, conversation and continuity of action are totally shattered. The action becomes symbolic of the moral disorder of the participants, and human behavior is seen to be the equivalent of the desolate ash heap presented in the chapter's opening paragraphs.

CHAPTER III

Moving from the second to the third chapter the reader goes directly from one party to another. The relation of any events that may have taken place between the two parties is postponed, so as to juxtapose Tom's gathering with Gatsby's, for the purpose of emphasizing the similarities and differences between them. This chapter is similar to the second in that its main purpose is to provide background, though this time it is the milieu of Jay Gatsby that is under scrutiny.

The opening paragraphs, describing a typical Gatsby party rather than a specific occasion, are much-acclaimed examples of Fitzgerald's style and his ability to create a mood. Gatsby's blue gardens are full of guests moving with the beauty and unreality of moths, but when the gardeners appear, the fragile atmosphere of Sunday night is broken by the reality of Monday morning. Here the author's style is made appropriate to the presentation of illusory beauty suddenly shattered by reality, which is one of the main themes of the entire novel.

Gatsby's mansion has been turned into a gigantic machine that processes guests just as the machine in his kitchen processes fruit, and the emphasis is on the apparent meaninglessness of the whole cycle. The seemingly purposeless nature of Gatsby's parties is seen in the description of the guests, most of whom have not been invited and who accept his hospitality without even meeting him. "Introductions forgotten on the spot" and the empty, sham enthusiasm of the women define the nature of the party; splendid in appearance, it is merely an illusion created by money. The most prominent colors at the party are silver and gold (or yellow), representing the wealth that has made it all possible, just as it has reconstructed "the Merton College Library," full of impressive volumes that are unread and uncut.

Gatsby emerges as a gifted theatrical producer with an unlimited budget, and the clear implication is that the host, like the party he gives, is a splendid, expensive illusion. His famous smile, the most effective of his props, is a masterpiece of illusion, but when it vanishes Nick is left facing an "elegant young roughneck" whose manners and speech are no longer consistent with the atmosphere he has created.

Just as the illusion created by the Gatsby smile dissipates when the gesture ceases, the artificial gaiety of the party disappears when the orchestra goes home and the guests begin to depart. Husbands and wives turn on one another to the point of physical violence, and one guest manages to wreck his car in a ditch. The main point of the accident is the sheer carelessness and bizarre lack of understanding shown by the driver and the other guests, symbolic of their profound moral carelessness and opacity. "Owl-Eyes" and his advisers cannot understand that the wheel is broken off from the car and therefore it cannot be driven, in the same way that they have no real understanding that acts have consequences for which one has to be morally responsible.

This minor accident is also of special importance because it is related to the argument about "carelessness" between Nick and Jordan later in the chapter and because it foreshadows the accident that kills Myrtle. It is fitting that the automobile, the symbol of material wealth in America, should be the instrument that ultimately leads to Gatsby's death.

During the party and at its end the quality of Gatsby most insisted upon is his isolation; alone and apart, he observes the festivities but never enters into them. Later he stands before his vast, empty house, formally saluting the departing guests, recalling the way he stood alone at the end of the first chapter. His isolation is an indication that while he regularly "dispenses starlight to stray moths," he is doing it for a purpose. It is all part of the plan for achieving his dream, a means to an end, and therefore he keeps apart from the corruption of the means, consecrating himself to the purity of the goal.

The remainder of the chapter is devoted to filling in the details of Nick's day-to-day life and to expanding on his affair with Jordan, a main device for bringing the narrator into the novel's action and illustrating the development of his character. Nick is confronted with Jordan's incurable dishonesty, a problem related to the "carelessness" of her driving and corresponding to the moral carelessness shared by Tom and Daisy as well. At this point Nick states that Jordan's dishonesty makes no difference to him, although later he will be faced with the difficult decision of what to do about her. It is indicative of Nick's ethical responsibility that before he can allow himself to become involved with Jordan he must free himself from a "vague understanding" he shares with a girl in the middle west.

CHAPTER IV

The opening sentences of the fourth chapter continue the wild speculation about Gatsby's identity, signaling that the main concern of the chapter will be to elaborate on this mysterious figure. But first Nick presents his fascinating list of Gatsby's guests, in a passage that rates among the best in the novel. The vulgarity of such names as S. W. Belcher, the Smirks, Miss Haag, and James B. ("Rot-Gut") Ferret, combined with the briefly noted activities of those named, gives a portrait of Jazz Age society. The names are written in the margins of an old, disintegrating railroad timetable, an ideal symbol of ephemerality, and it is important that the timetable is in effect July 5, 1922. July Fourth is of course the great American holiday, and so these are the people who appeared the day *after* the declaration of American independence. They represent what has become of American idealism in a corrupt age.

In America the automobile ranks first among status symbols, and Gatsby's gorgeous machine is the *ne plus ultra* of automobiles. "Swollen" with protuberances and of "monstrous" length, it is an overblown absurdity created by wealth to fulfill the American dream of personal material success. Later, it is also the fatal car that kills Myrtle Wilson and leads indirectly to Gatsby's own death. Here the reader can see Fitzgerald's sense of careful construction at work in the use of the symbolic automobile to support the thesis that an ideal based on materialism alone is ultimately destructive.

The autobiography Gatsby gives Nick is revealing in its comical vulgarity. Voluntarily cut off from his real past and left to create a personal history to fit the image he wishes to project, Gatsby invents an adolescent dream history, borrowed from sentimental romances and documented with realistic props. But like the parties, Gatsby's autobiography is brought into being solely for the purpose of attaining his goal, and therein lies the essential purity of the man. All that he has done, despite its vulgarity and obvious falsity, has been directed toward a single, transcendent ideal, and this lifts Gatsby above the world of sordid materialism into a sphere where he merits Nick's admiration.

On their trip into New York, Nick and Gatsby drive over a symbolic landscape. First they pass through the desolation of the valley of ashes, representing reality, and the sense of corruption is heightened by the encounter with the policeman. Then, moving across the bridge, they pass into a world of unreality in which the city appears to be made of sugar lumps because of its white beauty and its lack of real substance. The hearse they pass is premonitory: two death cars speed along the same road in view of the city of illusion. The encounter with the wealthy Negroes in the limousine is intended to emphasize the infinite possibilities of the city of "wild promise," the symbol of all America. The ridiculous ostentation of the Negroes is of course parallel to Gatsby's own, and their appearance has been foreshadowed by Tom's racist worries in the first chapter. Here the city of wild promise and wonder is shown to produce only dead men and ludicrous displays of affluence.

Nick receives a hint in the form of Meyer Wolfsheim of how Gatsby really amassed his wealth. This bizarre denizen of the twenties underworld, with his cuff links made of human teeth and his comical nostalgia for "the night they shot Rosy Rosenthal," serves to give another insight into the corrupt reality on which the attainment of Gatsby's dream is based.

Jordan Baker's account of Gatsby's early relationship with Daisy is first of all illustrative of Fitzgerald's narrative technique. While the main body of the book moves along in chronological progression in the novel's present, there are also interspersed flashbacks into Gatsby's past. These are of varying length, appear in non-chronological order, and are presented by various characters (Gatsby himself, Jordan, Wolfsheim, Mr. Gatz). In this way the author presents a series of fragments that ultimately piece together the story of Gatsby's life and serve to explain the already established facts of his existence in the story's present. The method itself is dramatic and economical, and is evidence of the extremely careful construction of this short novel.

Daisy's maiden name is "Fay," a synonym for "fairy," and this suggests her ethereal, insubstantial quality, as does the color white which is always associated with her. Her characteristic indecision and irresponsibility come out in the story of her brief faithfulness to the departed Gatsby and her marriage to Tom Buchanan the day after she drunkenly declares she has changed her mind. Later in the novel she reverts to loving Gatsby again, but in the same way the pressure of circumstances overcomes her feeling for Gatsby and brings her back to Tom.

The marriage of Tom and Daisy is put under critical scrutiny, and Fitzgerald paints a picture of idyllic marital bliss in the same paragraph with the evidence of Tom's immediate infidelity. The Buchanans have drifted from Santa Barbara to Cannes to Deauville to Chicago in a way that is symbolic of the moral rootlessness of the very rich, and Jordan hints at the possibility of infidelity on Daisy's part, an anticipation of the affair with Gatsby. Like all the contemporary songs recorded in *The Great Gatsby*, "The Sheik of Araby" has a special significance; in a sense, Gatsby *is* the sheik, about to invade Daisy's world and (hopefully) carry her off.

Most important is Jordan's revelation that Gatsby bought his house just to be across the bay from Daisy. This suddenly shows that the hidden motivation of Gatsby's "purposeless splendor" is to capture the woman who has come to represent his ideal. Thus the relevance of the epigram by "Thomas Parke D'Invilliers" (actually Fitzgerald himself) is made clear:

Then wear the gold hat, if that will move her;
    If you can bounce high, bounce for her too,
Till she cry "Lover, gold-hatted, high-bouncing lover,
    I must have you."

Gatsby believes he can win his woman with wealth, that he can attain the ideal she stands for through material affluence. The irony is that Daisy is unworthy of the vision, and even if she were worthy, it is doubtful that Gatsby could hold her with the "vulgar, meretricious beauty" that is his only attraction.

The exchange between Nick and Jordan raises some problems about Nick's own character. Jordan supports the Daisy-Gatsby affair on the grounds that "Daisy ought to have something in her life," and Nick goes along with the idea of arranging the meeting. Also he continues to become more involved in what is clearly a sexual affair with Jordan. These details make Nick a more "human" character and illustrate the extent of his "tolerance."

CHAPTER V

With the long-awaited meeting between Daisy and Gatsby the plot nears its climax. Gatsby comes into possession of the dream toward which he has shaped his entire life, and the remainder of the book is largely an analysis of the disintegration of that dream.

Even while the dream is being realized there are signs of the inevitability of its destruction, as is especially evident in Gatsby's vulgarity. As the chapter opens he wants Nick to accompany him to Coney Island, and Nick has noticed that the guests at Gatsby's own parties conduct themselves according to the standards of behavior of an amusement park. As a member of the established American aristocracy of wealth, Daisy could never live with a man who existed on Gatsby's social level, just as Tom could never marry Myrtle Wilson.

Gatsby's unawareness of the norms of behavior appropriate to Daisy's society is also evident in the open reward he offers Nick for setting up the meeting with Daisy. He does this in the naive expectation that Nick will accept the offer, without realizing how his friend would feel to be made, in effect, a pimp. This shows how alien Gatsby is to any system of established ethical values; he is not guilty of deliberately breaking a code of ethical conduct, but simply ignorant that such a code even exists.

Gatsby appears for the crucial meeting in a white suit, a silver shirt, and a gold tie, which is implicitly contrasted to Tom's traditional attire so much admired by Myrtle. Again, silver and gold are the colors of wealth, and Gatsby's sartorial splendor is as vulgar and *nouveau* as his car, his house, or his lavish entertainments. A display of wealth without tradition simply is not sufficient for permanent entry into Daisy's world.

During the tea Gatsby's behavior borders on the tragi-comic; he glares soulfully, stalks about "as if he were on a wire," and behaves in a manner that is entirely theatrical. Nick points out that he is conducting himself like a little boy, and in a sense that is precisely what Gatsby is. His romantic, adolescent quality is both the reason for his downfall and the key to his ability to maintain the purity of his vision. While on the one hand he lacks the maturity to realize that Daisy is unworthy of his ideal and that she can't be obtained by money alone, he also retains a youthful capacity for faith and wonder that enables him to remain a romantic idealist in a spiritual waste land.

In a way Gatsby's career resembles that of the unfortunate brewer who built his feudal home. Both put all their energy into building a dream that is inconsistent with the realities of American society, and each went into an immediate decline when that dream was shattered by reality.

Daisy's guided tour through the mansion is a key section of the novel. The culmination of Gatsby's years of dreaming, it is also his first revelation that once the goal is attained, the means to it become purposeless. When Daisy enters the house everything in it must be re-evaluated, and mere material objects lose their reality in her presence because she is representative of a higher, transcendent reality toward which all of Gatsby's possessions are dedicated.

Gatsby's shirts are the central symbol of the chapter. Far more than mere garments to wear on one's back, they are among the "enchanted objects" created by money, significant only inasmuch as they contribute to winning the ideal vision. This spiritual significance invests the shirts with a meaning that transcends their physical existence and gives them a "sacred" quality like that of the green light. Unlike the Buchanans, Jordan, or Myrtle, Gatsby never uses material objects in a selfish way, merely for his own enjoyment. Everything he owns exists only for the attainment of his vision, and this sets him apart and makes him spiritually greater than the materialistic society in which he lives.

When one's whole being has been dedicated to achieving a single goal, the attainment is as much a defeat as a victory, for there is nothing beyond it to conquer. Therefore Gatsby begins "to run down like an over-wound clock" when it seems that Daisy is finally his, and the tremendous intensity of the quest dissolves in the realization of the attainment. Now that he has Daisy herself the green light is no longer an enchanted object, since there is no use for the symbol when one has the real thing. As the significance of the green light vanishes forever, Gatsby begins to realize in a bewildered way that *no* material object, not even Daisy herself, can replace the ideal he has created through "the colossal vitality of his illusion," and so his personal tragedy is that he can find no real correlative to his vast spiritual capacities. Gatsby's personal dilemma is a specific example of a general American problem, for no amount of material affluence could ever match the pure, romantic promise of the new world, whose sugar-cube cities and fabulous wealth are illusions because they cannot fulfill the dream on which the republic was founded.

Gatsby is most attracted to Daisy's wonderful voice because that is the most unrealistic thing about her. It is an illusion that hides what Nick has called her basic insincerity, but its enchantment holds Gatsby more than any physical aspect of the woman, because it is her one quality that can sustain his own illusory vision. As the chapter closes in the symbolic setting of "the hour of profound human change," Gatsby resists the change that threatens his dream now that the goal is achieved, and clings to the promise represented by Daisy's voice.

CHAPTER VI

This chapter completes the presentation of Gatsby's personality and explains his development by flashbacks into two critical periods of his past. This narrative method is far more effective than a simple chronological account of Gatsby's life, not only in that it contributes a certain amount of suspense, but principally because it gives the reader the details of Gatsby's past *after* he has been fully presented in the novel's present. The effect of this is to undercut the glamorous illusion of what Gatsby seems to be by suddenly exposing what he really is, a movement roughly similar to the impending destruction of his dream by the realities of the world in which he lives. The real history narrated by Nick is of course harshly dissonant with the information Gatsby himself has provided in Chapter IV, and the negation of that romantic story at this point is an anticipation of the destruction of the whole illusory fabric of Gatsby's life.

The visit of the young reporter and the further speculation about Gatsby's antecedents prepare the reader for what is to follow. The most important point in the story of Gatsby's youth is that he hasn't changed in any essential way since he was a boy of seventeen. At that point in life or even earlier, James Gatz had invented Jay Gatsby, "and to this conception he was faithful to the end." Here is the basis of his naive, romantic capacity for wonder, as well as for the peculiarly immature quality of the life he has made for himself. Both his strength and his weakness, the purity of his faith and his incredible self-delusion, stem from a kind of arrested development.

It is important that in his imagination he has completely dissociated himself from the world of his parents. Like the little boy in Fitzgerald's short story "Absolution," Gatsby has invented a totally new person, and in becoming that new person he has lost the heritage of a historically oriented way of life, creating instead a new world of pure wealth and illusion. On another level, Gatsby's history is that of the archetypal European in the new world, voluntarily cut off from his outworn cultural antecedents and dedicated to the American dream of achieving an ideal state by amassing unlimited personal wealth.

Dan Cody, the source of Gatsby's "singularly appropriate education," is an American archetype in his own right. Having attained the American ideal of infinite and instant wealth, Cody makes the move from west to east, like all the characters in *The Great*

Gatsby, and there he plays the role of *nouveau riche* with a vengeance. Unlike Gatsby he has no transcendent purpose to which to dedicate his wealth, and so he devotes the rest of his life to moral degeneration and endless, aimless drifting aboard his yacht. Here again is the theme that wealth without a worthy purpose or a viable heritage is ultimately self-destructive.

The brief confrontation of Tom and Gatsby at the latter's home serves to contrast the two men even further. By this time Gatsby's affair with Daisy has become well established, and Gatsby is uneasy around Tom, though he treats him hospitably, in marked contrast to Tom's brutal, uncaring attitude toward George Wilson. While they accept Gatsby's hospitality, Tom and his friends contrive to cut him socially, another instance of the way everyone except Nick *uses* Gatsby. Hundreds come to his parties, but almost no one will attend his funeral. Gatsby's own lack of social *savoir-faire* is again brought out; he would like to attend the dinner party to which he seems to be invited, and he can't see that the invitation doesn't extend to him. Tom's hypocrisy is also much in evidence in the statement of his belief that "women run around too much these days."

Gatsby's party shows the beginning of the dream's disintegration. Unlike his first party, this one has a new unpleasantness or harshness because it is being evaluated according to Daisy's standards rather than those of West Egg. As long as the illusion of gaiety was self-contained and unself-conscious it could be maintained, but now that it is judged by an outsider to Gatsby's world the illusion must inevitably break down. In the same way, the illusion of Gatsby's whole being is viable only as long as it is based on an unattained ideal, but now that the ideal has been attained in the form of Daisy, the vision itself must be destroyed.

Daisy is a stranger to the gaudy world of the West Eggers and is displeased with every aspect of the party but one: she is drawn to the scene between the movie director and his star. Those two figures form a kind of theatrical set-piece, an island of lovely and totally unreal gesture in the midst of a sea of emotion, and Daisy's fascination is a sign of her "insincerity," her desire to *play* at life rather than participate in it to the point where she is responsible for her actions. Play-acting and empty gestures are invariably more attractive to her than genuine emotions.

Tom comes off badly at the party, abandoning Daisy to pursue another woman and then becoming hypercritical of Gatsby's "menagerie" of guests, which is an especially ridiculous pose in view of his own little party in Chapter II. The Buchanans' disapproval echoes the theme of old money and new, showing again that Daisy could never be happy in Gatsby's environment. She is also worried about losing her lover to some "authentically radiant young girl," a fear that underscores the inauthenticity of Daisy's own radiance.

The chapter ends with a conversation and a flashback into yet another part of Gatsby's life, both of which are very important in understanding the specific nature of his dream. He wants to do away with time in order to obliterate the four years Tom and Daisy have been married, and he has absolute faith in his ability to repeat the past, despite Nick's statement that this is impossible. This romantic disregard for reality is at the center of the American dream as well as Gatsby's own, in the belief that sufficient wealth would enable one to recapture and "fix" forever, the ephemeral, illusory qualities of youth and beauty. Yet even as Gatsby speaks of his dream he walks down a path covered with the symbols of reality. The fruit rinds, discarded party favors, and especially the crushed flowers are evidence that the past cannot be fixed and maintained forever, that the party must always end sometime, leaving a rather unpleasant residue. The symbols of the pleasure and gaiety of the night before are the garbage of the morning after.

The beautiful description of Daisy's "incarnation" as the dream presents the moment when Gatsby's vision takes on the seed of its own destruction. Before this time the dream remained pure and unlimited because it was not involved with a specific material phenomenon, but remained wholly spiritual. Gatsby sees that the ladder to the stars could be scaled "only if he climbed *alone*" (italics supplied), but when he weds the dream to the woman, combining his "unutterable visions" and her "perishable breath," a new and immediate sense of limitation is created, and the dream shrinks into Daisy. Just as at the end of Chapter V, when Gatsby finally attains the vision, the setting here emphasizes that it is a time of change and excitement. The atmosphere is charged with a special aura that signals a major change in the course of Gatsby's life.

On hearing all this Nick is reminded of something he can't quite recapture, and he is affected by it. What stirs him is the archetypal nature of Gatsby's dream, the fact that it parallels the nearly forgotten idealism that is the basis of the American experience.

CHAPTER VII

This chapter, the longest of the novel, opens with the information that Gatsby's "career as Trimalchio" is over. Trimalchio, a character created by the Roman satirist Petronius, is a vulgar upstart whose low origins are shown by his extravagance and ostentation, and Fitzgerald considered various alternate titles for *The Great Gatsby* that involved the name of this figure. But although Gatsby's career is over in the respect that he no longer gives his lavish entertainments now that there is no need for them, he maintains his dream to the very end, even after Daisy is lost to him. In this he is more than a "Trimalchio" because his vulgarity is the more superficial aspect of his personality.

Fitzgerald never reveals the details of the relationship between Daisy and Gatsby very explicitly because their affair is of no real interest in itself, but only in relation to Gatsby's dream. Instead there are only hints, such as Gatsby's statement that Daisy often visits in the afternoon, and Nick's remark that in the present hot weather it makes little difference whom one makes love to. The hot weather is constantly emphasized; it is a correlative for the buildup of dramatic tensions that explode the plot in this climactic chapter.

In many details the opening scene in the Buchanans' home is a duplicate of the similarly placed scene in Chapter I. Jordan and Daisy occupy the same enormous couch, both in their white dresses, and again Tom is called away by a telephone call from his mistress.

This careful repetition of physical detail suggests that despite Gatsby's intrusion into Daisy's life, the basic situation of the Buchanans is really unchanged from what it was at the opening of the novel.

Daisy's actions are as indiscreet as her voice, and her kissing Gatsby while Tom is momentarily out of the room is illustrative of her characteristic carelessness. It shows that loving Gatsby is just a game to her, to be played on her own terms. Later, when the men try to force her to come to a real decision, she chooses Tom. Her little girl is as unreal to her as it is to Gatsby himself; Daisy has no real feeling for the child, whom she calls a "dream" and parades before company in the same way Tom shows off his horses. Gatsby of course finds it difficult to adjust to the child's presence, since nothing could be more out of harmony with his dream of returning to the past than the existence of Pammy Buchanan.

As the conversation progresses, the personalities of Tom and Daisy are more firmly established. The vacuousness of their lives is alluded to again in Daisy's query as to what they will do in the future; with unlimited wealth and very limited personal resources, life is indeed empty for them. Daisy's remark that Gatsby resembles an advertisement is a key to her whole attitude toward him. She doesn't want him for what he is, but for the superficial illusion of what he represents. In modern culture it is in advertising that the material aspect of the American dream is most prominently displayed. There eternal youth, beauty, and wealth are permanently exhibited, and it is this aspect of Gatsby that most attracts Daisy.

Tom reacts to the realization that Daisy has declared her love for Gatsby like a man whose possessions are suddenly threatened, looking at her "as if she had just recognized her as some one he knew a long time ago." The overt comparison between Tom and Wilson, the two cuckolds, emphasizes the difference between them: Tom is in a panic lest his wife slip away from him, while Wilson becomes ill with a sense of his own guilt, blaming himself for Myrtle's infidelity. It is characteristic of Tom's brutal sensibilities that he is relieved to find that Daisy has only "loved" Gatsby for the past five years, since physical intercourse is the only relationship his mind is capable of appreciating. Despite his shabby affair with Myrtle he has the hypocrisy to equate the threat to his own marriage with a universal breakdown of family life.

When Gatsby describes Daisy's voice as being "full of money" he defines the charm she holds for him. In American culture as well as Gatsby's personal dream, the ideal is always bound up with wealth. Therefore, to be properly qualified as the goal of Gatsby's aspirations, it is essential for Daisy to be the "golden girl" of popular romance, the princess who marries the young man of humble antecedents.

The previous confrontations between Tom and Gatsby have all taken place in the homes of either one or the other. However, now that they have become open antagonists they move to the "neutral ground" of a hotel suite. Fitzgerald creates a tense, uneasy atmosphere, opening the dialogue with a long and irrelevant conversation about the Man from Biloxi, and the background sound of Mendelssohn's Wedding March contributes an ironic counterpoint to the marital disharmonies of the Buchanans. Then the pace changes abruptly as Tom turns on Gatsby, and all the studied inanity disappears as the tension mounts.

This is the moment of Daisy's betrayal of Gatsby's vision. She would like to preserve the status quo and continue to enjoy both the security of being Mrs. Buchanan and the attentions of Gatsby, so she first tries to head off her husband, and failing that she interrupts Gatsby and pleads to go home. To her, any alternative is better than being forced to come to a decision, but Gatsby insists, because the total attainment of his dream depends on Daisy's public repudiation of her husband. Not only must she say she doesn't love Tom, but in order to wipe out the last four years she must claim she never loved him. This last item causes her to break down and turn to her husband, and from that point on Tom is in complete control of the situation. By the time Tom brings out his strongest weapon, the source of Gatsby's wealth, Daisy is lost to Gatsby forever, despite his frantic efforts to revive the "dead dream." Tom sends Daisy home with Gatsby as a gesture of confidence, to illustrate his victory.

Nick's sudden preoccupation with the fact that it's his thirtieth birthday seems at first to be out of place, but actually it is a very relevant detail. The age of thirty is symbolic of the passing of youth, and so the turning point in Nick's life occurs simultaneously with the turning point in Gatsby's career, the death of his youthful dream.

Besides its obvious function as the mechanism that resolves the plot, the destruction of Myrtle Wilson also forces Nick to come to full moral responsibility. Myrtle's violent death is the ultimate piece of "carelessness" of the Buchanans, and it causes Nick to abandon them, and Jordan as well. Jordan has remained nonchalant and unaffected by the day's events. After seeing Myrtle's mangled body she is still anxious to go to dinner, coaxing Nick to accompany her by pointing out that "it's only half-past nine." The coldness of her personality has been evident all through the novel, but here it is finally enough to drive Nick away.

Gatsby's pathetic vigil is the final proof of the inviolability of his dream. Even after Daisy has betrayed him he insists on remaining to protect her, and it is this largeness of character that causes Nick to side with him against the selfishness of the Buchanans. Ironically, Gatsby's vigil is over an empty room, just as his dream is built around an empty person. While he watches over nothing, Tom and Daisy are drawn together for self-protection, in the manner of conspirators.

CHAPTER VIII

At the opening of Chapter VIII a new mood is established. The mournful groan of the foghorn is a foreshadowing of Gatsby's death, as are Nick's nightmares. Nick's new sense of responsibility is evident in his desire to warn Gatsby, for in this act he definitely takes sides, committing himself to his friend. Gatsby can't run away as Nick advises, because that would constitute an admission that his dream really has been destroyed. Instead he clutches at a last, desperate hope that Daisy might still choose him, excusing her behavior of the previous day with the explanation that under Tom's pressure she hardly knew what she was saying.

In the flashback to Gatsby's relationship with Daisy five years before, the elements that have contributed to Gatsby's dream are enumerated again, showing youth and beauty to be inextricably bound up with wealth. Daisy's porch is "bright with the bought luxury of star-shine," and she "gleams like silver" with a beauty imprisoned and preserved by money.

It is important that Gatsby's commitment to Daisy is described in terms of a quest for a grail. The pursuit of his ideal has often been associated with religious imagery: he appears in the attitude of a worshiper in Chapter I, his mind is compared to the mind of God, the sidewalk stairway to the stars is a kind of Jacob's Ladder, his vigil over Daisy is "sacred," and now he is implicitly compared to a knight in pursuit of the Holy Grail. On one level this imagery suggests the spiritual nature of his quest, but on another, it implies that his faith is misplaced because his goal is nothing more than Daisy Buchanan. By extrapolation from Gatsby to America as a whole, one can say that the spiritual capacities of the nation are misplaced in the pursuit of material wealth and that the result is a national delusion which parallels Gatsby's own.

Daisy is seen in a more sympathetic light at this point in her life, appearing as a weak, overprotected person rather than a vicious one. In a sense Gatsby tricked her by letting her assume he was her social equal, and her decision to marry Tom was just a response to her lack of inner resources. She had to have her life "shaped" by some outside force, and unable to wait for Gatsby, she allowed herself to be overcome by Tom Buchanan. This is almost precisely what she has done again five years later, in the previous chapter. Wavering in her judgment she puts up a brief struggle and then surrenders herself to the strongest force.

Gatsby's remark that even if Daisy did love Tom, "it was just personal," shows the intense, transcendent quality of his vision. To him, love is more than a personal relationship because it goes beyond the people involved and becomes fused with the ideal. This is why he can keep his dream alive even after Daisy has failed him on a personal level; his "incorruptible dream" is so strong it can sustain itself in the face of anything.

The autumnal atmosphere, with its falling leaves and plans for draining the pool, signals that the end is near. The novel begins with Nick coming east in the spring, reaches its climax in the heat of the summer, and closes with the falling leaves of autumn. Thus the Gatsby story is laid out against a symbolic background of the seasons, each corresponding to a phase in the culminating episode of his life.

Nick's statement that Gatsby is "worth the whole damn bunch put together" indicates that the narrator has developed to where he can no longer reserve judgment; it is the sum of what he has learned in the course of his stay in the east. Despite his total disapproval of Gatsby's vulgarity and self-delusion, Nick respects him for the strength and unselfish nature of his idealism.

The long conversation between Michaelis and George Wilson serves to advance the plot and to give a portrait of the state of the ordinary man in the waste land, which is one of almost total delusion. Wilson has no religion, and his lack of spiritual values results in his wasting away to the point where there isn't even "enough of him for his wife." In this blindness he mistakes the eyes of Dr. T. J. Eckleburg for those of God, and he ends his life after killing the wrong man under the encouragement of his wife's lover. He is so much a part of the waste land that he is described as an "ashen, fantastic" figure, a part of the material world that has lost its essential reality by giving up its spiritual element.

Gatsby dies with his faith still alive, awaiting the improbable phone call from Daisy. The main message of Nick's speculation as to whether he kept his faith to the end is the statement of how grotesque and in fact unreal the material world is without the necessary spiritual element. In a larger sense, then, Gatsby's unshakable faith in his dream has been an affirmation of the richer, more essential part of life, rather than a negation of reality, and so despite his limitations he emerges as the one admirable character besides Nick.

CHAPTER IX

The final chapter illustrates Nick's full assumption of responsibility and ends in an overt connection between Gatsby's career and American history. Nick takes care of the details of Gatsby's funeral partly because there is no one else to do it and partly because of the "scornful feeling of solidarity" between Gatsby and himself. Unlike Wolfsheim, Klipspringer, and all the people who used Gatsby during his life, Nick is the only person besides "Owl-Eyes" who has enough real feeling for the man to take an interest in giving him a decent burial.

Against Nick's responsibility is placed the irresponsibility of Tom and Daisy, who had fled to New York even before Gatsby was murdered, carelessly leaving the chaos they created to be straightened out by others. Tom is filled with self-pity over the loss of his mistress, and gushes with sentimentality over a box of dog biscuits, but has no qualms whatever about having sent Wilson to murder Gatsby. The fact that Daisy has never told him the truth about the accident and that he has therefore caused a man to be murdered by mistake is part of the "grotesque" carelessness Nick perceives to be pervading eastern society. It is on a par with his imaginary vision of four men delivering an unknown, drunken woman to the wrong house, and not even caring.

In contrast, Nick expresses a desire to "leave things in order" rather than just hoping they will take care of themselves. After the telephone conversation with Jordan in the previous chapter he could easily have let their relationship resolve itself, but instead he insists on clearly terminating the affair, although he still feels strongly attracted to the girl. Accused of carelessness, he points out that he is thirty, five years too old to lie to himself by taking pride in his honesty. His recognition that even he has not conducted himself with complete honesty is a step forward from his statement at the end of Chapter III that he is one of the few honest people he has known.

The two carefully juxtaposed flashbacks into Gatsby's past, one from Wolfsheim and the other from Henry C. Gatz, are revealing in that neither gives a full picture of the Gatsby the reader has come to know. Wolfsheim's statements about the adult racketeer are followed immediately by the portrait of young Jimmy's all-American boyhood, but the essential element of the man, his intense spirituality, is missing. Here Fitzgerald shows that neither Gatsby's father nor the man who "made" him really understands what he was. A full understanding can only be acquired by piecing together the various fragments of his life as they have been presented.

Mr. Gatz's copy of Gatsby's "schedule" is especially important in that it places his son squarely in the American tradition. Written on a copy of the adventures of Hopalong Cassidy, another typically romantic American figure, Gatsby's program for self-improvement is right out of Franklin's *Autobiography,* even in some of its smallest details (electricity, inventions). Because of its content and what it is written on, the schedule illustrates two basic qualities of the American hero: hard-working ambition and a romantic thirst for adventure.

The way in which Wolfsheim's description of Gatsby is followed immediately by Mr. Gatz's account of his boyhood is structurally and thematically related to a similar juxtaposition a few pages later. Nick first describes Gatsby's funeral and then jumps directly to an account of the promise of his own youth, with his prep school days corresponding chronologically to Gatsby's boyhood. As in Mr. Gatz's account, Nick's central theme is the "identity with this country," the relation of youthful ambition and promise to the spirit of America itself. Gatsby's corruption is thus related to the historical corruption of the American spirit, the destruction of the nation's early idealism by its involvement with a materialistic ethic.

The main theme becomes more explicit in the novel's final paragraphs, in which Gatsby's green light is compared to the "green breast of the new world." The word "breast" suggests that for the early explorers the promise of America was like that of a woman, just as Gatsby's personal dream is incarnate in a woman. Here Gatsby's dream is universalized by its identification with the wonder of the newly founded republic, and so Gatsby himself is enlarged into a mythic figure whose career and fate represent that of America itself. In part, this is the reason for his isolation and his total break with his personal past; to be magnified in this way he must be set apart from the rest of society, above the shabby medium in which he tries to realize his dream. The word "pandered" connotes the corruption of "this last and greatest of human dreams," the final moral that the ideal can never be realized in the gross materialism that has made a moral valley of ashes of the green freshness of America.

NOTES ON MAIN CHARACTERS

NICK CARRAWAY

Although Nick is not the titular hero of the novel, his importance as the narrator and as a functioning character makes him almost as much a central figure as Gatsby himself. *The Great Gatsby* begins and ends with Nick, and on one level the intervening events tell the story of his own development.

At the outset Nick is already a sophisticated observer of character, but he is inclined to reserve his personal judgments, remaining uninvolved in the sense that he is unwilling to act on what he perceives to be the faults of the other characters. For example, he realizes that Jordan Baker is an incurable liar and that this is an indication of a basic defect in her personality, similar to the brutality and irresponsibility of Tom and Daisy, but at this point he is willing to "tolerate" her defects. As Nick realizes, he is "both within and without," never totally a part of the action around him, yet acting as a mainspring for that action by bringing Daisy and Gatsby together.

Nick's sense of humor functions as an indication of his objectivity. At the same time he is interacting with the other characters, his rather impersonal judgments of them are expressed in his humorous assessments of their actions. Good examples are when he points out Tom's "transition from libertine to prig," or when he reflects on Gatsby's first, ludicrous version of his past, "leaking sawdust at every pore as he pursued a tiger through the Bois de Boulogne."

When he witnesses the reaction of Jordan and the Buchanans to Myrtle Wilson's death, Nick reaches the symbolic age of thirty and quickly develops a full sense of moral responsibility. He realizes he can no longer tolerate the moral vacuousness that lies beneath the wealth and sophistication of eastern society, and so he returns to the middle west, after carefully fulfilling his personal responsibilities.

Nick's personal development is allied to his roles as narrator and judge. With a sense of morality based on his midwestern heritage, he can perceive the flaws in Gatsby's dream and the basic differences that make Gatsby a better person than the Buchanans. Functioning as Fitzgerald's voice in making his ultimate value judgments, Nick realizes that an ideal based on materialism alone is a corruption rather than a fulfillment of the American dream, and yet that the selfless devotion to even a corrupt ideal is morally superior to the complete selfishness that motivates everyone except Gatsby.

JAY GATSBY

Unlike Nick, Gatsby does not develop in the course of the novel. He cannot, because his whole life is devoted to the fulfillment of a romantic dream he created at a very early age, and by its very nature his dream requires an adolescent faith amounting to self-delusion to sustain it. His personal vision is based on the illusory belief that time can be "fixed" and the past can be repeated forever. The means by which this goal is to be attained is wealth, and so Gatsby's vision is like the American dream itself, the delusion that youth and beauty can be perpetually recaptured if only one can make enough money. The overt connection between Gatsby's vision and the American dream is in the identification of his boyhood ambitions with those of Benjamin Franklin, and also the comparison of his capacity for wonder with that of the early explorers, overcome with the promise of the new world.

As a romantic dreamer who seeks to fulfill his ideal by amassing wealth as a racketeer, Gatsby is a symbol for the whole American experience. The corruption of his dream by adopting materialism as its means and illusory youth and beauty as its goal is the corruption of American idealism, which becomes the empty promise of advertising—a vast, vulgar "universe of ineffable gaudiness."

In the end Gatsby is destroyed by his illusions just as surely as the American landscape has been converted into a ghastly "valley of ashes."

DAISY BUCHANAN

Daisy is a portrait of the American woman of her class, and in some ways she is not unlike Fitzgerald's wife, Zelda. In fact her remark that she had hoped her daughter would be "a beautiful little fool" is almost precisely what Zelda said after giving birth to her own daughter, Scottie, and the parallels between the Daisy-Gatsby courtship and Fitzgerald's own have already been noted in the Introduction.

Like all of Fitzgerald's women, Daisy is beautiful, enchanting, and hollow; the emptiness of her character behind a facade of charm betrays Gatsby's dream and leads indirectly to his death. From the beginning it is clear that despite her outward contrast with her husband's hulking brutality, she and Tom are really partners in a "secret society" of established wealth, and that she could never leave Tom for Gatsby.

This is not to say she doesn't love Gatsby, or at least the grandiose gesture he has directed toward her. Both at the time of her marriage and her affair she is drawn toward him, but in both cases her lack of inner resources permits Tom to effectively overcome any attachment she has to her lover. Like Zelda's brief affair with the French aviator, Daisy's involvement with Gatsby ends abruptly when her husband steps in.

Her seeming emotion is only the illusion of love, just as her voice gives only the illusion of sincerity; behind it is a complacent smirk. Because of her wholly illusory quality she fits in perfectly as the incarnation of Gatsby's dream, which is built on the illusory premise that money alone can fulfill an ideal. This means to attaining the dream corrupt the goal, and in her actual emptiness Daisy represents the corrupted goal itself, entirely meretricious behind the beauty of its promise.

TOM BUCHANAN

As the representative of the morality and values of the established rich class, Tom is contrasted both with Gatsby's idealism and Nick's personal integrity. Having neither quality makes him admirably equipped to succeed in a world in which idealism is impossible and integrity is passé. While Gatsby dies and Nick returns to the middle west, Tom is able to stay in the moral waste land without any of Nick's feelings of "provincial squeamishness" over what has happened.

All Tom's feelings and actions are self-directed. He entertains his guests by showing off his possessions, including his mistress, and he experiences anxiety only when he sees he is about to lose Daisy and Myrtle. Incapable of guilt over causing Gatsby's death, he wallows in self-pity over the loss of his mistress.

It is possible to suspect Fitzgerald of a certain amount of admiration for Tom in spite of the overt censure the man receives. He is direct and capable of taking decisive action, and even Nick is a little awed by the power of his physique and the extent of his wealth. In the same way, the author finds something attractive in the protected snobbery of Daisy's girlhood, and so to some extent one can detect Fitzgerald's own ambivalent attitude toward wealth in the characterization of the Buchanans.

JORDAN BAKER

Jordan exists mainly as a device to draw Nick into the plot. Her romance with Nick receives relatively little exposition, but it is carefully set up to parallel the affair of Gatsby and Daisy. Jordan is identified as a member of Daisy's class both in her appearance and her moral irresponsibility, and the two affairs develop simultaneously up to the time of Myrtle's death. At this point, Nick's rejection of Jordan (he leaves her at the Buchanans' house) is contrasted with Gatsby's deluded devotion, shown by his vigil over the house, and the insight that protects Nick is contrasted with the lack of insight that leads to Gatsby's destruction.

CRITICAL REVIEW

IDEAS

Out of Fitzgerald's presentation and analysis of the lives of Gatsby, Nick, and the Buchanans comes the final theme that American idealism has been corrupted by adopting materialism as its means. The substitution of attractive but false goals, represented by Daisy, as the fulfillment of the historical promise of America, has changed the new world (the east) from a "fresh, green breast" to a grotesque waste land where only the morally irresponsible can hope to survive. Gatsby's destruction shows that those who try to maintain an idealism based on purely materialistic values are doomed by their self-delusion, and George Wilson's unfortunate career illustrates the fate of the common man in the waste land. Because he remains faithful in the end to the "provincial" moral values of the middle west, Nick is able to avoid personal destruction, but he is also unable to continue living in the east and must return to the traditional moral environment of his home.

The corruptive effect of wealth is shown by the conflict between the established rich and the newly rich, represented by the East Eggers and West Eggers. Hypocritical and morally careless, the East Eggers naturally regard any change in the social hierarchy as a threat to the entire structure of society, as brought out by Tom's alarmist remarks about the dissolution of the family and eventual intermarriage between black and white. The West Eggers live in a world of ostentatious vulgarity, resulting from the adoption of wealth as their only standard. While society is changing, as shown by the Negroes in their limousine, the nature of the change is that the lower orders are trying to adopt the values and standards of the privileged classes, which are false to begin with. Thus both classes are equally corrupt, and East Egg and West Egg are virtually identical when seen from a distance.

SETTINGS

The degradation of the promise of America is implicit in the historical reversal of east and west. When the early explorers (the

Dutch sailors) escaped the corruption of the old world to establish a new ideal, they traveled from east to west. But now that the ideal has been corrupted people travel from west to east, attracted by the wealth and sophistication that masks the moral desolation of their goal. As Nick points out, "Tom and Gatsby, Daisy and Jordan and I, were all Westerners," and in moving to the east they move from a world of stable values into a moral vacuum symbolized by the "valley of ashes."

On a smaller scale, the physical settings are also important in establishing the identities of the main characters. As was pointed out in the Commentaries, the homes of Gatsby, Tom, and Nick all correspond to their class status and characteristics. Gatsby lives in an enormous imitation palace, representative of the ostentatious vulgarity of the newly rich. Tom has a Georgian Colonial mansion that befits his status as one of the established rich, and Nick's conservative, middle-class bungalow among the mansions of the wealthy corresponds to his own status in the society in which he moves.

The seasons serve as a backdrop to the drama of Gatsby and Nick. As the year progresses from spring at the beginning of the book to fall at the end, Nick's moral sense becomes established, coming to fruition in his final actions in the autumn. Gatsby's personality cannot develop in this way, and like the fallen leaves that float beside his body in the pool, he comes to destruction with the end of the year.

TECHNIQUE AND STRUCTURE

All of the foregoing aspects of characterization, presentation of ideas, and use of settings properly come under the heading of technique and contribute to the book's structure. They are given independent consideration for the sake of convenience, but it must be kept in mind that all aspects of a successful novel become integrated into the total structure to create its unity, and that achieving this unity is the goal of the novelist's technique.

The technical aspect that makes *The Great Gatsby* the best organized of Fitzgerald's novels is the use of Nick Carraway as a first-person narrator who is himself involved in the action. This method lends compactness and unity to the novel, since the reader is confined to what Nick can experience and hear. In addition, Nick is endowed with a personality that compels him to make overt moral judgments of the other characters and himself, and so the ideas conveyed in these judgments come from a person involved in the action and thereby seem to arise spontaneously from the action itself. This makes for a more unified, self-contained effect than if the final moral judgments were imposed from the outside by the author.

While Nick's own story develops chronologically in the novel's present, the background information necessary to understanding Gatsby is presented in a series of flashbacks that appear in non-chronological order and are related by various characters. This technique helps to integrate Gatsby's history with the development of the plot and contributes to the overall dramatic effect of the novel. It is far more effective first to present a mysterious character and then to gradually unveil his past than it would be to give all the information about him in the beginning. Further, the gradual revelation of Gatsby's past corresponds to the destruction of the dream which is his sole reason for being, so that the narrative technique parallels the course of the main action.

The essentially dramatic quality of the novel is also evident in Fitzgerald's use of presentation rather than summarized narrative for key scenes. In each instance in which an important plot development takes place, the characters are shown in action, revealing their personalities directly to the reader. The most important single use of this technique is in the climactic scene in Chapter VII, though the various parties and gatherings are all effectively presented.

In analyzing Fitzgerald's technique one should consider what he leaves *out* of the book as well as what he includes. Instead of presenting a connected, day-by-day narrative, he jumps from scene to scene, focusing only on those few incidents which best support the total structure. For instance, Nick is ostensibly in the east to learn the bond business, yet there are only the vaguest passing allusions to his business activities, since these have no real place in the book's structure. Again, while Gatsby has become wealthy through his racketeering, the one part of his life that isn't much elaborated upon is the actual process of accumulating his wealth, for the author is interested in the consequences of having money rather than the process of obtaining it. An omission that bothered Fitzgerald himself is that once Daisy and Gatsby have been brought together, there is no relation of the details of their affair until the point at which it ends. One explanation for this omission is that Daisy's superficiality and Gatsby's adolescent attitude toward her would make their relationship a mundane thing. More important, it is the consequences of the relationship that are significant rather than the relationship itself, and of course these consequences are fully explored.

All of these omissions demonstrate Fitzgerald's concern for creating a tightly knit, highly organized narrative structure, in which every scene and detail contribute to the total effect and in which extraneous material is carefully avoided.

Another aspect of Fitzgerald's technique is his use of juxtaposition. He often puts two scenes or passages together for the sake of a more dramatic comparison, as in the transition from Chapter II to Chapter III, when the reader moves directly from Tom Buchanan's party to Gatsby's. A juxtaposition of a slightly different kind occurs in the final chapter when Wolfsheim's revelations about Gatsby are followed immediately by those of Mr. Gatz, providing two contrasting views that serve to emphasize the corruption of Gatsby's purpose. Again, the abrupt transition from Gatsby's funeral to Nick's prep school holidays serves to contrast present realities with the promise of youth, supporting a main thematic concern of the final chapter.

STYLE

All of the techniques discussed above are stylistic matters as well, but it would be more convenient to confine this section to Fitzgerald's prose. Always highly polished and often richly poetic, his prose style is at its best in the descriptive passages, especially when he is trying to create a mood. While the dialogue is always spare and convincing, the descriptions are fully developed and often luxurious with images of color and sound, as when Nick describes the atmosphere of one of the parties: "The moon had risen higher, and floating in the Sound was a triangle of silver scales, trembling a little to the stiff, tinny drip of the banjoes on the lawn."

The silver moonlight in this sentence is one of many examples of Fitzgerald's use of images of color. Silver and gold (or yellow), the colors of wealth, recur again and again, associated especially with vulgar displays of affluence. Daisy's color is white; she wears white dresses and recalls her "white girlhood," and this use of color helps to characterize her as the unattainable "enchanted princess" who becomes incarnate as Gatsby's dream. Green is very significantly associated with both the green light and the "green breast of the new world," uniting the hope and promise of Gatsby's dream with that of America itself.

SYMBOLISM

The Great Gatsby is rich in symbolism which functions on several levels and in a variety of ways. One of the most important qualities of Fitzgerald's symbolism is the way it is fully integrated into the plot and structure, so that the symbols seems naturally to grow out of the action rather than existing as mere abstractions.

Some symbols are used primarily as devices for characterization, such as Wolfsheim's cuff links, Gatsby's spectacular library of uncut books, and Tom's repeated gesture of physically shoving other people around. Other symbols, such as Gatsby's car, have a function in the plot as well as a more abstract significance. The faded timetable on which the names of Gatsby's guests appear serves to characterize the whole social class rather than a single person, and the names themselves are symbolic in their connotations.

The major symbols such as the ash heap, the green light, and the east and west have already been discussed at length. These are invested with meanings that go beyond the concerns of plot and characterization, standing for the main ideas of the novel and relating them to a general criticism of American culture.

There are a few minor characters whose main significance is symbolic, in particular Dan Cody. While Cody's importance in advancing Gatsby's career is undeniable, the man had died before the time of the main action. He serves as an American "type," a man who struck it rich and was incapable of using his new-found wealth for anything but self-destructive purposes.

Finally, the action itself has a symbolic dimension. The various parties reflect a moral as well as physical chaos, and the careers of the main characters symbolize the novel's controlling ideas. Gatsby's career is made to transcend the physical environment of the twenties, becoming a metaphor for the fate of American idealism in the modern world.

REVIEW QUESTIONS

1. Discuss the implications of Gatsby's failure to develop in the course of the novel. (Notes on Main Characters)

2. Compare the relationship between Gatsby and Daisy to that of Jordan and Nick. (Chapter VII; Notes on Main Characters)

3. What is the effect of gradually revealing Gatsby's true past and how does this method relate to the overall ideas of the book? (Technique and Structure)

4. Working from the "present" time of 1922, prepare a chronology of Gatsby's life by ordering the various fragments of his past.

5. Compare Gatsby's *use* of money with that of Tom Buchanan and Dan Cody. (Chapter VII)

6. Discuss the significance of Gatsby's boyhood program for self-improvement. (Chapter IX)

7. Outline the course of Nick's development from "tolerance" to full moral responsibility.

8. What are the advantages or effects of using Nick as a first-person narrator? (Chapter I; Technique and Structure)

9. Nick suddenly remembers his thirtieth birthday at a seemingly peculiar point in the novel. Why? (Chapter VII)

10. How do Tom and Daisy represent the morality of the established-rich class?

11. Discuss the effects of Daisy's "incarnation" as Gatsby's dream. (Chapter VI; Ideas)

12. How do Daisy's reasons for marrying Tom foreshadow her later betrayal of Gatsby? (Chapter VIII; Notes on Main Characters)

13. Gatsby says that Daisy's voice is "full of money." How does this relate to his conception of her as his dream, and to the novel's theme? (Chapter VII)

14. Why does Daisy call her little girl a "dream," and what is Gatsby's reaction to the child? (Chapter VII)

15. Do you agree that Dan Cody's function is mainly symbolic? How about Pammy Buchanan? (Chapter VII; Symbolism)

16. What function, if any, does Michaelis serve? (Chapter VIII)

17. What do you understand to be the purpose of the religious imagery used to describe Gatsby's quest? (Chapter VIII)

18. Choose any example of Fitzgerald's use of color and relate it to the ideas of the novel. (Style)

19. Some of the novel's symbols have *not* been discussed in the Notes, for example the obscene word chalked on Gatsby's house which Nick erases (Chapter IX). Discuss the meaning of this symbol. Can you relate it to any others?

20. Compare the homes of Gatsby, Nick, the Buchanans, and the Wilsons. How does each relate to the personality of its owner? (Chapter I; Settings)

21. How do the various contemporary songs relate to the ideas of the novel?

22. Choose any particular setting and discuss its symbolic function.

23. What is the symbolic use of east and west? Why do all the main characters travel from west to east? (Ideas)

24. Analyze the description of any one of the parties or gatherings, showing how it is used in the characterization of the participants.

25. Choose any instance of juxtaposition and explain its use. (Chapters III, IX; Technique and Structure)

SELECTED BIBLIOGRAPHY

I. Biographical Material

Eble, Kenneth E. *F. Scott Fitzgerald.* New York: Twayne Publishing Co., 1963. A short critical biography designed "to bring out the defining characteristics of Fitzgerald's writing."

Fitzgerald, F. Scott. *Letters,* ed. Andrew Turnbull. New York: Charles Scribner's Sons, 1963. A mine of biographical information.

Mizener, Arthur. *The Far Side of Paradise.* Boston: Houghton, Mifflin, 1951. The first full biography of Fitzgerald; thorough, detailed, and containing much useful critical material.

Piper, Henry Dan. *Scott Fitzgerald: A Candid Portrait.* New York: Holt, Rinehard, and Winston, 1963. Specialized, critical, and especially useful for background material.

Turnbull, Andrew. *Scott Fitzgerald: A Biography.* New York: Charles Scribner's Sons, 1962. Another major biography briefer and less critical than Mizener's, but very readable.

Wilson, Edmund, ed. *The Crack-Up*. New York: New Directions, 1945. Autobiographical essays by Fitzgerald and other useful material.

II. Critical Studies

Hoffman, Frederick J., ed. *The Great Gatsby: A Study*. New York: Charles Scribner's Sons, 1962. A collection of important essays and other material on *The Great Gatsby*.

Kazin, Alfred, ed. *F. Scott Fitzgerald: The Man and His Work*. Cleveland and New York: World, 1951. An anthology of earlier essays (to 1945), mostly by those who knew Fitzgerald.

Miller, James E. *F. Scott Fitzgerald, His Art and Technique*. New York: New York University Press, 1964. Traces Fitzgerald's growth as a conscious, professional artist, emphasizing *The Great Gatsby* as his major achievement.

Mizener, Arthur, ed. *F. Scott Fitzgerald: A Collection of Critical Essays*. Englewood Cliffs, N.J.: Prentice-Hall, 1963. Essays on Fitzgerald's career and work with a section on *The Great Gatsby*.

III. Individual Essays and Articles

A full, reliable bibliography of periodical articles on Fitzgerald appears in the *Modern Fiction Studies,* VII (Spring, 1961), 82-94. This can be brought up to date with the annual bibliography for American literature in *Publications of the Modern Language Association*. The following articles, some of which appear in the anthologies above, are especially useful in studying *The Great Gatsby*.

Brewly, Marius. "Scott Fitzgerald's Criticism of America," *Sewanee Review,* LXII (Spring, 1964), 233-46. Discusses the theme of *The Great Gatsby* as the withering of the American dream.

Dyson, A. E. " 'The Great Gatsby': 36 Years After," *Modern Fiction Studies.* VII (Spring, 1962), 162-67. A good analysis of the meaning of Gatsby's dream.

Fussell, Edwin. "Fitzgerald's Brave New World," *English Literary History,* XIX (December, 1952), 291-306. Another examination of Gatsby's dream.

Hanzo, Thomas A. "The Theme and Narrator of 'The Great Gatsby,' " *Modern Fiction Studies,* II (Winter, 1956), 183-90. A study of Nick Carraway's development.

Ornstein, Robert. "Scott Fitzgerald's fable of East and West," *College English,* XVIII (December, 1956), 139-43, Discusses the meaning of the east-west contrast.

Stallman, Robert W. "Gatsby and the Hole in Time," *Modern Fiction Studies.* I (November, 1955), 1-16, An analysis of Nick's characterization.

Thale, Jerome. "The Narrator as Hero." *Twentieth Century Literature,* II (July, 1957), 69-73. Nick as the real hero of *The Great Gatsby.*

NOTES